Canada's Pioneers Table of Contents

Canada's Pioneers Curriculum Overview	2
Canada's Pioneers Teachers Tips	3
Canada's Pioneers Unit Assessment Strategies	4
Centre Based Activity Cards	5
Research Reporting Opportunities	6
Canada's Pioneers Parent Letter	7
Sample Morning Messages	8
Canada A Better Life	12
Create A Family Tree	14
Early Settlers In Upper Canada	15
Clearing The Land	17
Aboriginal People Helped Pioneers	19
Jerky and Pemmican	22
Early Settlers in Western Canada	23
Western Settlement: Red River Colony	26
Settlements in Eastern Canada	28
Pioneer Health	29
Pioneer Fun	31
Inside A Pioneer Home	32
Growing and Finding Food	34
Pioneer Life: Storing Food	37
Pioneer Life: Preserving Food	39
Comparing Pioneer Day Eating to Modern Day Eating	41
Pioneer Dried Apple Treats	42
Pioneer Butter Making	43
Pioneer Cheese	45
Pioneer Villages	47
The General Store	49
Pioneer Occupations	51
Pioneer School Time	53
Homemade Fiddle	55
People and Places in a Pioneer Village Word Search	56
Pioneer Farm Animals and Crops Word Search	57
Comparing Pioneer and Modern Day Chores	58
Pioneer Farm Crops	59
The Gristmill: Grinding Grain Into Flour	62
Spinning Flax Thread	64
Sheep Wool	65
Pioneer Paper Quilt	66
Pioneer Activity Cards	67
Canada's Pioneers Home Study	70
Canada's Pioneers Unit Test	73
Self Evaluation: What I did in the unit	76
Rubric for Self Assessment	77
Student Assessment Rubric	78
Student Evaluation Sheet	79
Student Certificates	80

GeoWat innovative teacher publishing ©2003

Canada's Pioneers: Curriculum Overview

This unit covers the following learning expectations:

- Identify the countries where pioneers came from.
- Identify reasons why early settlers came to Canada.
- Investigate why children's families have come to live in Canada and where their family originates.
- Describe the influence of Aboriginal peoples and pioneers in the area of farming methods.
- Identify the contributions of Aboriginal peoples to pioneer settlement.
- Describe the major components of a pioneer village or settlement.
- Describe the lifestyles of male and female pioneers and the various roles of individuals in a pioneer settlement.
- Compare and contrast the lives of pioneer and present day children.
- Compare and contrast life in a pioneer settlement with that in their own community.
- Compare and contrast buildings in a pioneer settlement with those of the present day.
- Compare past and present techniques of storing and preserving food.
- Use appropriate vocabulary and terminology.

Canada's Pioneers Teacher Tips

What I Think I Know / What I Would Like to Know Activity

A great way to engage children in a new theme is to ask them what they think they know about a subject and what they would like to know about a subject. This activity can be completed as a whole group brainstorming session, in cooperative small groups or independently. Once children have had a chance to contemplate the theme, all information is combined to create a class chart that can be displayed in the classroom. Throughout the study, periodically update the children's progress in accomplishing their goal of what they want to know and validate what they think they know.

Morning Messages

Morning Messages are intended to provide students with interesting facts about the theme they are studying while also arranging teachable moments in the use of punctuation. Morning Messages are an excellent way to get the learning going when the students enter in the morning. There are numerous Morning Messages included with this unit. The Morning Messages are written in a letter format. There are several ways to present a Morning Message to your class:

Whole Group: Rewrite the morning message on a large sheet of chart paper and allow students to come look for the "mistakes" in the letter. Then as a whole group read the letter together and use it as a springboard for a class discussion.

Individually: As children enter the classroom, give them a copy of the Morning Message and have them fix the "mistakes". The children practise reading the message with a friend until the class is ready to correct the morning message as a group. Use the Morning Message as a springboard for discussion.

Reading Cloze Activities

Cloze activities are not only useful for learning new information, but can be also used to practise reading skills. The children practise reading each cloze page individually or with a friend and finally with the teacher. Initial the page if reading is satisfactory.

Word List

Word Lists create a theme related vocabulary. Word Lists should be placed on chart paper for students reference during writing activities. Encourage students to add theme related words. In addition, classify the word list into the categories of nouns, verbs and adjectives.

Canada's Pioneers: Unit Assessment Strategies

Learning Inventory Unit Test

At the completion of the unit children participate in a paper/pencil learning inventory quiz to test knowledge of concepts covered during the unit. The learning inventory includes true and false, and some written answers.

Home Study

The purpose of the project is designed so that children will have better understanding of how their daily lives are different yet the same as pioneers.

Constructed Response- Learning Logs

Learning logs are an excellent means for children to organize their thoughts and ideas about the concepts presented. Grammar, spelling or syntax should not be emphasized. The student responses give the teacher opportunities to plan follow up activities that may review and clarify concepts learned.

Learning log entries may be done on a daily basis or intermittently depending on scheduling. Entries should be brief. Time allotted for completion should be less than fifteen minutes. Entries can be done with a whole group, small group or an individual.

Learning logs can include the following kinds of entries:
- Direct instructions by the teacher;
- Key ideas;
- Personal reflections;
- Questions that arise;
- Connections discovered;
- Labelled diagrams and pictures.

Learning logs can take the form of:

- Journal;
- Entries in a classroom portfolio;
- Reflective page.

Student Centred Parent Conferences:

Children have an opportunity to share their portfolio work with their parents, as well as demonstrate their knowledge.

Self Assessment:

Children are asked to evaluate themselves in different areas such as group skills, oral presentation skills and to reflect on what they learned.

Centre Based Activity Cards

Learning centre activity cards provide optimal opportunities for children to practise interacting and sharing ideas with their peers in positive ways. Centre based learning also promotes children in taking ownership for their learning.

In order for run successful learning centres. Good planning on the part of the teacher is essential. Follow these steps:

First: Examine your timetable and decide on one time block to be devoted consistently to learning centre time.

Second: Decide how many centres will be set up during learning centres and what they will be.

Third: Store what is needed for each activity in their individual bin. In this way, centres are organized and ready to go. Each centre bin should include:
- An activity card describing the activity;
- All materials needed to complete the activity for each child;
- A sample of completed work to show students.

Fourth: Introduce and explain the expectations of each learning centre to the class. This is the time to teach any specific skills, needed to complete an activity. In addition, review how many students are at each centre.

If a learning centre approach is new to your classroom, balance your activities so that some activities need minimum teacher direction, such as a construction toy centre where children build a pioneer village. This will allow the students an opportunity to:

- Learn routines in how to move through each centre;
- Know the number of children allowed at a centre;
- Practise working independently and with others.

As the teacher, circulate among the centres encouraging children:

- To be self-directed learners;
- To use their peers as a resource for help;
- To work at their fullest potential.

Research Reporting Opportunities

Research reporting opportunities are an excellent way to ensure children have experience in reading informational text and restating what they have learned in their own words. Set up a pioneer theme related centre by preparing a special table with subject related materials including, books, tapes, magazines or artifacts.

When introducing the children to the use of non- fiction books as a source for their research writing, discuss the different parts usually found in a non-fiction book.

The Title Page: Here you will find the book title and the author's name.

The Table of Contents: Here you will find the title of each chapter, what page it starts on and where you can find specific information.

The Glossary: Here you will find the meaning of special words used in the book.

The Index: Here you will find the ABC list of specific topics you can find in the book.

Next, discuss with the children the criteria of a good research project. It should include:

1. Interesting facts;
2. The use of proper grammar and punctuation;
3. The size of print so that it is easy to read from far away;
4. The use of good details in the colouring and the drawing of pictures.

Canada's Pioneers: Parent Letter

Dear Parents and Guardians,

In our next unit of study, your child will be focusing on the pioneer settlers of Canada. Your child will have the opportunity to identify the countries of origin of settlers and describe their life and contributions. A comparison will be made of the life of early pioneers and their own lives. The contributions of Aboriginal peoples will also be explored.

This study will be used as a springboard for numerous activities. In addition, students will be given the opportunity to complete a home study. Look for the information package soon!

Families may contribute to our study by lending any resources, such as CD ROMS, books, newspaper articles, collections, tapes, Internet sites etc.

Your family's enthusiastic participation in our class study is greatly appreciated.

Sincerely,

_____

Sample Morning Messages

Dear Pioneer Investigators,

Did you know That in 1824, more than 2000 people came from Ireland to settle in the area north of rice Lake, ontario? Eventually, these Irish settlers founded the city of peterborough. The government helped these Irish settlers by giving 100 acres of land to each family and to each person over 21 years of age? Each family also received enough salt pork, and flour to last many months. this food was very important to the irish settlers because. often they cAme to Canada with very little except the. clothes on their backs and needed time to establish their farms

Brainwork: Make a list of things you think are necessary in your daily life.

Dear Pioneer Experts

did you know pioneers had many chores in order to get ready for winter? October and November were usually very busy months for early settlers? Fruits And vegetables needed to be preserved and stored. candles for lighting needed to be made. Animals needed to be slauGhtered and preserved by smoking or salting for tasty winter meals. sometimes jobs were too big for one family, so a neighbourhood bee was held. Cornhusking, apple paring and quilting bees were just a few. after The Work the early settlers had a celebration.

Brainwork:
Make a list of things you need to be ready for winter.

Sample Morning Messages

Dear Pioneer Experts,

Did you Know before any settlers arrived, Aboriginal peoples lived in what is now canada for thousands of years? The early settlers or pioneers of Canada and Aboriginal peoples hAd different points of view about how the LAnd should be used. pioneers Thought the land should be divided and owned by individuals and forests cleared to make waY for permanent settlements? aboriginal people Thought the land was something to be shared and respected

Think about it!

Brainwork: Write a journal entry about why it is important to respect the earth.

Dear Pioneer Experts,

Did you know that most pioneers had to measure things by using different body parts such as hands, or the length of their foot? This was because rulers and other measuring devices were hard to come by. For example, when buying fabric you would ask for a cloth yard. A cloth yard was the length of the merchant's outstretched arm, from his nose to his thumb tip.

Brainwork:
Measure things around the classroom using your feet or hands.

Sample Morning Messages

Dear Western Homesteaders,

Did you know the journey by train from Quebec to western Canada took around four to six days? It was not an easy trip. Passengers had to provide their own food. The trains were often overcrowded with many delays. Once when the homesteader family arrived at a town close to their homestead they got off the train. They then bought a wagon and loaded up their belongings. They also bought supplies like food, clothing, seed, farm animals and tools.
Happy traveling!

Brainwork: On a map of Canada trace a route that settlers might have taken from Ontario to western Canada.

Dear Busy Pioneers,

Did you know working as a team was very important for pioneers? Pioneers worked together to help each other out. When groups of neighbours gathered, it was called a "bee." A "bee" was when a group of people got together to accomplish something. There were bees to build barns, clear land, plough fields or build fences. Women held special "bees" to preserve fruit and vegetables or to create beautiful warm quilts. After a "bee" people usually had a celebration and socialized.
Happy Work Bee!

Brainwork:
Think of a class project and work together to complete it.

Sample Morning Messages

Dear Pioneer Experts,

Did you know the first settlers in what is now British columbia came from Russia, Spain and England. They came to trade furs with the Aboriginal peoples who already had lived there? Not much time passed before many others Came to settle in British Columbia. Villages and Towns grew around permanent trading posts.

HappY Trading!

Dear Gold Lovers,

Did you know the discovery of gold along the fraser River on Canada's western coast caused many people to go there? ThousAnds of miners traveled to the Interior in the hopes of finding gold. Many people who came from California were born in China. These people became the first Chinese immigrants to British Columbia.

Happy Gold Rush!

Canada: A Better Life

Did you know the early settlers who made Canada their home are known as pioneers? People came to settle in Canada for many reasons. Some people came to settle here so they could freely practise their religion. Some people settled here because they did not like the way their home countries were run. People came to Canada for a better life.

Aboriginal peoples are the only people truly from the country we call Canada. All other Canadians have ancestors who decided to make Canada their home. Some Canadians have ancestors from early pioneer times. Some Canadians have grandparents or parents who moved to Canada. Some Canadians are newly arrived to Canada.

Think about it!

1. What are three reasons early settlers chose to come live in Canada?

_____

_____

_____

2. Discover what countries your family is originally from and why they chose to make Canada their home.

_____

_____

_____

Canada: A Better Life

1. Pretend you are moving to another country. What are ten things you would take with you?

2. What kind of feelings do you think an early settler had coming to Canada for a better life? Explain.

_____

_____

_____

3. Survey your classmates and find out where their ancestors are from. Make a list of the countries.

_____

_____

_____

Create A Family Tree

Trace how far back your family tree can go!

Where were you born? _____

From what parts of the world is your family from?

_____

_____

_____

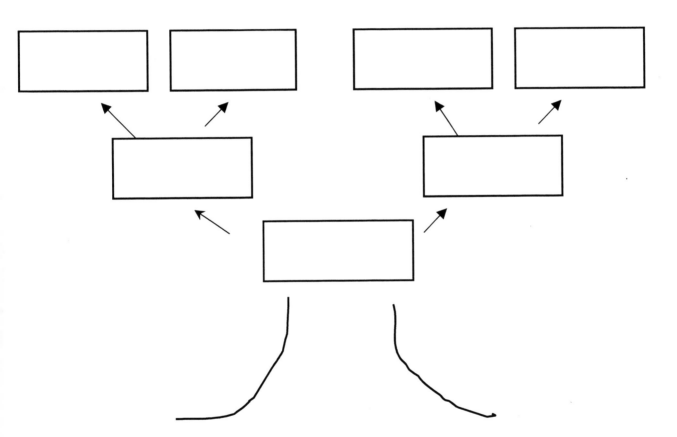

Share your finding with your classmates.

Early Settlers in Upper Canada

Did you know that southern Ontario, along the upper section of the St. Lawrence River, was once known as Upper Canada? In 1791, the old Province of Quebec was divided into Upper and Lower Canada. The Ottawa River was the boundary between these two areas. Many people came to settle in Upper Canada in the late 1700s and 1800s in search of a better life.

People who settled in Upper Canada came mostly from Great Britain, France, Scotland, Germany or other parts of Europe. Others who came to Upper Canada were from the United States and were called United Empire Loyalists.

The **United Empire Loyalists** were people who lived in the American colonies and were loyal to Great Britain. In 1776, the American colonies separated from Great Britain and became the United States. The United Empire Loyalists were unhappy about breaking their ties to Great Britain. As a result, they decided to move to Upper Canada for a new life.

United Empire Loyalists often brought slaves with them from the United States. In Upper Canada an important law was passed, that halted the selling of slaves. Upper Canada became a safe place for escaped or freed slaves from the United States. During the 1850s thousands of slaves escaped to Canada in order to live free. The **Underground Railroad** was a special secret organization that helped smuggle slaves to Canada.

Many people in Europe took very difficult trips across the ocean in the hope of a better life in Canada. This was because they led a hard life in their homeland. For example, during this time period there was a potato food shortage (famine) in Ireland. As a result, many Irish people starved, or became very ill and died. Many people were forced to leave their homes with very little to survive and nowhere to go. Many of these poor Irish farmers came to live in Canada.

Thinking about: Early Settlers in Upper Canada

A. Fill in the blanks using information from the reading.

Did you know that _____Ontario, along the upper

section of the _____, was once known as Upper

Canada?   In 1791, the old Province of Quebec was

_____ into Upper and Lower Canada. The

boundary between these two areas was the _____.

B. Answer the following questions using the information from the reading.

1. Where were the United Empire Loyalists from and why did they settle in Upper Canada?

   _____

   _____

   _____

2. Why did poor Irish farmers leave their home?

   _____

   _____

   _____

3. Explain why Upper Canada was a safe place for slaves.

   _____

   _____

   _____

Clearing the Land

Did you know that one of the first things an Upper Canada settler had to do was clear the forest? It was important to clear the vast amount of land quickly so crops could be planted. Often, clearing the land was something the settler had no experience doing. Sometimes a **"logging bee"** was held where other settlers came to help a new settler clear land.

The first step was to clear the underbrush or small bushes and trees. All the family members helped. The cut branches were dragged to a certain spot and stacked into piles to dry out for a few months. The brush was carefully burned once dried out.

As the underbrush was cleared the second step was to cut down larger and taller trees. The limbs and branches of these trees were cut off, dragged away and burned. The long sturdy trunks of the trees were cut into lengths and stacked. The logs were used to build a log cabin while the extra logs were sold for lumber or burned to make charcoal or potash.

The third step was to pull out the stumps of the trees. This was a difficult task and settlers often used oxen to pull tree stumps out of the ground. Sometimes the stumps of the trees were used to build stump fences so that animals could be kept away.

GeoWat innovative teacher publishing ©2003

Thinking about: Clearing the Land

1. Using information from the reading and your own ideas, explain why it was difficult for a settler to clear the land.

   _____

   _____

   _____

2. What was a "logging bee"?

   _____

3. Explain the steps in clearing land for crops.

   _____

   _____

   _____

   _____

   _____

   _____

   _____

   _____

   _____

Aboriginal Peoples Helped Pioneers

Did you know Aboriginal peoples helped Canada's pioneers? They showed the pioneers how to farm. They showed the pioneers how to make medicine. They showed pioneers how to survive Canadian winters. They also showed pioneers how to catch food and where to find other things to eat.

Many Aboriginal peoples were expert farmers and helped pioneers to best use the land. For example, the women of the Iroquois nation taught the early settlers of Upper Canada how to grow tasty corn. They showed the early settlers how to choose good kernels for planting and how to make the soil rich with fish fertilizer. The ripe corn was then ground to make flour for cornmeal. The Iroquois also taught the early settlers how to plant other crops such as pumpkins, beans and squash.

Aboriginal peoples helped pioneers cope with illness. They shared with the pioneers, ways of making medicine from plants, berries and herbs. They showed pioneers how spruce and juniper trees could be used to make a nutritious tea to prevent scurvy.

The early settlers were not used to the cold winters in their new home. Luckily, the Aboriginal peoples traded goods for warm outer clothing. Aboriginal peoples crafted warm vests, jackets, pants, coats and special shoes called moccasins using deerskin and other animal hides.

Aboriginal peoples demonstrated for pioneers how to make snowshoes to help walking in snow easier. Snowshoes were made with wooden frame that looked similar to a tennis racket and woven animal hide across the wooden frame to make a net. Aboriginal peoples showed the pioneers how to make toboggans too.

GeoWat innovative teacher publishing ©2003

Thinking about: Aboriginal Peoples Helped Pioneers

Using the information from the reading and your own ideas explain the importance of the Aboriginal Peoples' help to pioneers.

_____

_____

_____

_____

_____

_____

_____

Indicate if the statement is true or false.

1. Aboriginal peoples showed pioneers how to make toboggans.   True   False

2. Early settlers were used to cold winters.   True   False

3. Aboriginal peoples did not like to trade goods.   True   False

4. Many Aboriginal peoples were expert farmers and helped pioneers how to best use the land.   True   False

5. Aboriginal peoples helped pioneers cope with illness.   True   False

Thinking about: Aboriginal Peoples Helped Pioneers

Complete the chart using information from the reading.

Ways Aboriginal Peoples Helped Pioneers	Example
Farming	
Medicine	
Coping with illness	
Coping with winter	

Jerky and Pemmican

Did you know Aboriginal peoples taught early settlers different ways to preserve meat? For example, Aboriginal peoples taught early settlers how to make jerky. **Jerky** was made with dried meat strips. Meat such as venison, was cut into thin strips, smoked and then dried out in the sun. The jerky was stored in special birch-bark containers for many months without spoiling. Trappers or traveling settlers ate jerky on their trips since it was nutritious and lightweight.

Sometimes nuts, seeds or dried berries were added to powdered Jerky and mixed with melted fat. This recipe was called **pemmican**. Pemmican was rolled into balls and stored in a dry cool place. Pemmican was often added to dishes like boiled cornmeal to make a tasty porridge.

Think about it!

1. Aboriginal peoples taught early settlers to make _____.

3. Jerky was made using dried _____ strips.

4. Meat such as _____, would be cut into thin strips, smoked and then dried out in the sun.

5. Jerky was stored in special _____ containers for many months without spoiling.

6. Trapper or traveling settlers ate jerky on their trips since it was

   _____and _____.

7. Sometimes nuts, _____ or dried berries were added to

   powdered _____ and mixed with melted fat. This recipe

   was called _____.

Early Settlers in Western Canada

Did you know "**homesteading,**" describes turning free land given out by the government into farms? Many people came to build homesteads on the Canadian prairies in the late 1800s. The Railways and land companies persuaded people from eastern Canada, the United States, Great Britain and other parts of Europe like the Ukraine to come live in the west in the hope of a better life.

Aboriginal peoples lived on the prairies for thousands of years. Before western homesteaders arrived, the Aboriginal peoples lived a rich life. The Aboriginal peoples respected the land, and traded goods with each other.

Once the western homesteaders came, the open grasslands of the prairies were ploughed and became wheat fields of newly built farms. As a result, the millions of bison that once freely roamed the land almost disappeared.

Life was very hard for new homesteaders. Often a husband would arrive before his family to build a home. Farms or homesteads were set up at Red River and around trading posts through the west.

Homes were made from different materials. Some people who had trees on their land built log cabins. Some people made huts out of planks or wood from packing cases. Most often, homesteaders used sod to build their home. **Sod houses** were made from pieces of turf or sod cut from the ground. The sod was then turned grass side down and was used like bricks to construct walls. Inside the sod house, the walls were usually covered with cloth or paper. The floor was typically left as packed earth. A sod house roof was made with poplar poles and covered with hay. Sod homes were warm in winter, cool in summer and often leaked after a rainstorm.

Early Settlers in Western Canada

In comparison to Upper Canada, the prairies had very few lakes and rivers. Sometimes western homesteaders found fresh water in a nearby pond. Usually homesteaders dug wells to get water. The water was pulled up in pails with a rope and pulley. If there was no water source available a homesteader had to take a long trip to the nearest water supply and haul back barrels of water.

Define the following bolded words from the reading:

1. Homesteading _____

_____

2. Sod house _____

_____

How were the western prairies different from Upper Canada?

_____

_____

Brainwork:

❖ Create a research poster that tells ten facts from the reading.

Thinking about: Early Settlers in Western Canada

Create a poster to attract people to come and live on the prairies. Make sure your poster includes:
1. Two reasons to come live in western Canada.
2. Good detailed pictures and easy to read printing.

Western Settlement: Red River Colony

Did you know the Red River Colony was the first pioneer settlement in what is now Manitoba? The Earl of Selkirk founded the Red River Colony in 1812 and called it Assinboia. He was a Scottish noble who wanted a new home for farmers who had been forced off their lands in Scotland. The Hudson's Bay Company granted the land for the settlement to Earl Selkirk. The Hudson's Bay Company controlled most of what is now western Canada during that time.

Along with the Scottish farmers, many other people lived at the Red River Colony. Some people were French-speaking Roman Catholics called Metis. Other people who lived at the Red River Colony were "country born" English- speaking Protestants. The rest of the population was made up a group of Aboriginal families who gave up their traditional way of living to become farmers. Some retired fur traders also chose to live there.

In the beginning, life at the Red River Colony was very difficult. There were many disagreements and fights over the roaming bison between the fur traders already there and the new settlers. The settlers struggled to establish farms and wanted to hunt the bison. The fur traders did not like that. The Red River colony also suffered through natural disasters like the flood of 1826.

Travel to the Red River Colony was difficult. The only ways to get there was by dog sled, canoe or York boat. Eventually, Red River carts and the railway made access for travelers to the Red River colony much easier.

Brainwork: Find the Red River on a map of Canada.

Thinking about western settlement: Red River Colony

A. Fill in the blank using information from the reading.

1. The Red River Colony was the first pioneer settlement in what is now

   _____.

2. The _____founded the Red River Colony in

   1812 and called it _____.

3. He was a Scottish noble who wanted a new home for farmers who had

   been forced off their lands in _____.

4. The _____ granted the land for the settlement to
   Earl Selkirk.

5. The Hudson's Bay Company controlled most of what is now

   _____ during that time.

B. Indicate if the statements are true or false using information from the reading.

1. The settlers struggled to establish farms and wanted to   True False
   hunt the bison.

2. Travel to the Red River Colony was easy.   True False

3. Some people who lived at the Red River Colony were   True False
   "country born" English- speaking Protestants.

4. The Earl of Selkirk founded the Red River Colony   True False
   in 1912.

5. Red River carts and the railway made access   True False
   to the Red River colony much easier for travelers.

Settlements in Eastern Canada

New France

Did you know the early settlers in New France were mainly farmers? They were from the country of France and were known as **habitants**. They lived in what is now much of Quebec, Ontario and the Maritimes. They put down roots along the rivers of the St. Lawrence Valley where the soil was rich and suited to farming.

The King of France owned New France. The land was divided in to large sections called **seigneuries**. The person in charge of the seigneurie was called a **seigneur** and usually lived in a manor house. The seigneur was like the king of the land and allowed habitants to work and live off the land. In return, the habitants gave the seigneur their crops. On the property, there was usually a church and a gristmill for grinding grain into flour.

Maritimes Provinces

Did you know most of the early settlers in Nova Scotia came from either France or England? French speaking settlers were called **Acadians**. Later on new settlers came from Germany, Ireland, and Scotland. Many Empire loyalists came after the American war of Independence.

Define the following bolded words from the reading:

Habitants _____

Seigneuries _____

Seigneur _____

Acadians _____

Pioneer Health

Did you know pioneers did not know much about germs? Many pioneers believed that bathing too much washed away body oils that kept them from getting diseases. Pioneers did not know the importance of washing their hands!

 Did you know pioneers sometimes visited a blacksmith if they had a toothache? A blacksmith would pull the tooth out with a pair of tongs. Pulling out a tooth was very painful. There was no freezing or painkillers for the person.

Did you know pioneers believed that some sicknesses were caused by poison in the blood? To get better, pioneers would visit the barber for a bloodletting. Bloodletting was when a small cut was made in the sick person's neck or wrist. The blood was then drained into a bowl. Sometimes leeches or bloodsucking worms were used for bloodletting.

Did you know pioneers used honey as medicine? Honey helped soothe sore throats and coughs. Honey was mixed with hot water, and lemon. Honey was also used as a salve for cuts and scrapes.

Think about it!
1. Fill in the chart, using the information from the reading and your own ideas.

What did pioneers do if they were sick?	What do you do in modern days if you are sick?

2. What surprised you about pioneer health and medicine?

_____

_____

Thinking about: Pioneer Health

Write a letter to a pioneer friend to explain how keeping healthy is different in modern days.

Dear _____

_____

_____

_____

_____

_____

_____

_____

_____

_____

_____

_____

Pioneer Fun

Did you know early settlers had to make their own fun? Some games that pioneer children liked to play were the same as modern days. These games include skipping and ball games. In pioneer times, a ball was made using an inflated pig's bladder. Girls also liked to sing rhymes. Try out some of the following pastimes, and have your own pioneer fun. These games can be played with children or adults too.

Checkers
Play a game of checkers. Try to make your own board game and pieces using found materials.

Shadow Shapes
Pioneers liked to make animal shapes using their hands. Their hands would make a shadow on a wall in the firelight. See how many animal shadow shapes you can make and have a friend guess the animal.

Musical Chairs
Play a game of musical chairs. Ask someone to sing for the music.

Storytelling
Many pioneer families enjoyed sitting together listening to a family member's tale. Sometimes stories were true and had a lesson. Sometimes for fun, stories were spooky and scary. Try taking turns telling stories in a group.

Charades
Pioneers liked role- playing or pretending and having others guess what they were doing. Take turns pretending you are different people in a pioneer village, like a blacksmith.

Brainwork:
1. Make a list of modern day fun and pastimes.
2. How is it the same or different from pioneer times?

Inside a Pioneer's Home

The Hearth

Did you know early settlers used their fireplace or hearth for both cooking and heating? Fireplaces were usually made of stone, with a mantle made of wood. A stone chimney took away the smoke. The hearth was the floor of the fireplace and was made with large flat stones. The hearth was deep so it could hold andirons. **Andirons** were iron stands that were used to hold the logs for the fire. A shovel was kept nearby the fireplace so that ashes could be removed. An iron poker was used to move or poke the logs to help keep the fire going.

Early settlers used iron pots and pans to cook with in the fireplace. A bucket of water was kept near the hearth, in case a fire got out of control.

Lighting

Did you know candles were the main source of light for pioneers? Some candles were made from beeswax. Some candles were made from tallow. **Tallow** was made using melted fat from pigs, cows or other animals. The animal fat was boiled in water, and then strained to rid of any dirty substances. Straining was done several times to make sure the tallow was as pure as possible. Sometimes wild ginger or other fragrant herbs would be added to the fat to give it a sweeter smell.

Next, twisted cotton cords were dipped into the hot tallow. Once the tallow cooled, the cord was redipped and cooled until a candle formed. Another way candles were made was to stretch cotton cord through a tin or wooden mould. The cotton cord was secured with a knot, at the pointed end, and to a stick at the other end. Melted tallow was left to cool and harden inside the mould. Candles were kept on candlesticks and in tin or glass lanterns.

Thinking about: Inside a Pioneer Home

A. Using information from the reading, connect the phrases to make true sentences.

1. Fireplaces were   to cook with in the fireplace.

2. Andirons, were iron stands   source of light for pioneers.

3. Tallow was made   usually made of stone.

4. Early settlers used iron   using melted fat from pigs,
   pots and pans   cows or other animals.

5. Candles were the main   used to hold the logs for the
   fire.

B. Using the information from the reading, define the following words.

Tallow _____

Andirons _____

C. Indicate if the following statements are true or false.

Some candles were made from beeswax.   True   False

An iron poker was used to move or poke the logs   True   False
to help keep the fire going.

Early settlers used their fireplace for heating only.   True   False

A bucket of water was kept near the hearth, in   True   False
case a fire got out of control.

A stone chimney helped keep the smoke inside   True   False
the home.

Pioneer Life: Growing and Finding Food

Did you know pioneers spent much of their time growing, and finding food? Pioneers cleared land to grow crops like wheat, and corn. Pioneers grew vegetable gardens with things like cabbage and onions. Pioneers raised livestock like sheep, chickens and cows. Pioneers hunted for wild game like deer, bear, turkey, and wild pigeons or fished. Pioneers also picked wild berries, fruits, vegetables, herbs and nuts. Honey, and maple syrup was used to sweeten foods.

Planting crops took much time and great effort year round by the whole family. First, the land was cleared. Second, seeds like wheat, oat, corn and barley were planted. Third, pioneers waited over time, hoping for a good mixture of weather so their crops could grow. Fourth, when ripe, the crops were harvested and milled. Gardens provided pioneers with yummy vegetables like potatoes, carrots and beans. These vegetables were eaten fresh, or stored and preserved. Herbs like thyme, sage and dill were also grown in the garden and gave food flavour to food.

Pioneers raised livestock to provide food and other things for the family. Pigs provided meat to make salted pork. The soft fat from the pig called lard was used to make candles and soap. Cattle provided milk to make butter and cheese. Oxen and horses were used to pull ploughs, wagons, carriages and sleighs. Sheep provided meat and wool to make yarn for clothing. Chickens provided eggs. Geese provided goose feathers to make soft pillows, and cozy mattresses.

Brainwork:
❖ Create a research poster to tell about the importance of livestock on a farm.

GeoWat innovative teacher publishing ©2003

Pioneer Life: Growing and Finding Food

Pioneers hunted in the woods and fished in streams for food. This helped to give variety to their diet. Pioneers hunted and snared using muskets, traps or nets. Wild game like venison, rabbit and even squirrels made tasty meals. Birds like quail, partridges, pigeons, grouse and duck were delicious. Fish like salmon, perch and herring were yummy fresh, dried or smoked.

The Aboriginal peoples taught the pioneers which wild berries, plants and fruits were safe to eat. Dandelion greens were eaten and made into dandelion wine. Fiddleheads, blackberries, mushrooms and even wild rice from the shallow parts of lakes were picked.

Maple syrup and sugar was used to sweeten foods.
Pioneers learned from the Aboriginal peoples how to collect sap from maple trees in the early spring and boil it to make maple syrup or maple sugar. First, a hole was made in a maple tree to collect maple sap. Next, a wooden tube was hammered into the hole. The wooden tube was called a spile. Under the spile, a bucket caught the watery sap drippings. Then the sap was boiled and run through a woolen cloth to remove impurities.

When pioneers discovered a honey bee tree, they were very excited. White sugar was expensive to buy and making maple syrup was hard work. Honey bee trees were found by following the path of bees as they went back to their hive. Once found, the beehive was left alone until it was full of honey. In the fall, the pioneer would go back to the hive with crocks and other containers to carry the honey. Wet leaves were burned over coals by the hive to make the bees sleepy and less likely to sting. The honeycomb and the sweet honey was taken home. Honey was used to sweeten food, and the beeswax was used to make candles.

Thinking about Pioneer Life: Growing and Finding Food

Using information from the reading, fill in the chart.

Types of pioneer crops	Things grown in a vegetable garden	Types of livestock	Names of animals and fish hunted by pioneers	Things picked in the wild by pioneers.

List six interesting facts you learned from the reading.

_____

_____

_____

_____

_____

_____

Brainwork:

❖ Create a research poster describing how to make maple syrup.
❖ Create a research poster to tell about a honey tree.
❖ Pioneers made almost all their food from scratch. Write a paragraph about how modern days are different.

Pioneer Life: Storing Food

Did you know one of the biggest hurdles early settlers had was making food last throughout the seasons? Pioneers did not have refrigerators to keep food fresh. Instead, pioneers used root cellars, springhouses, wells and icehouses to store food.

 A root cellar was a cool place where pioneers could store fruits and vegetables. A **root cellar** was an underground room underneath the kitchen or a room built into the side of a hill. Root cellars usually had stonewalls. Potatoes and other root vegetables were stored in a root cellar.   In the summer, milk and butter could be kept in a root cellar to keep from spoiling.

A **springhouse** was a shed built on top of a running spring. Usually butter and cream were stored in crocks and jugs and placed into the cold spring water. Sometimes pioneers kept food in pails deep inside a well.

An **icehouse** was a shed filled with blocks of ice. During the winter months, pioneers cut blocks of ice from a frozen lake or river. The blocks of ice in the icehouse, helped store food in the summertime.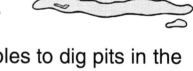

Early settlers also learned from Aboriginal peoples to dig pits in the ground.

Brainwork!

1. Pioneers used an ice house.
   In modern days we use a _____.

2. How is storing food easier in modern days?

_____

Thinking about Pioneer Life: Storing Food

One of the biggest hurdles for pioneers was to make food last throughout the seasons. Explain.

_____

_____

_____

Explain how pioneers used the following things to store food.

Root Cellar

_____

_____

_____

Ice House

_____

_____

_____

Spring House

_____

_____

_____

Pioneer Life: Preserving Food

Did you know food was preserved in pioneer times by being pickled, salted, smoked or dried?

Food was dried on a rack in the warm sun, or hung near a fire. Fresh fruits like apples or peaches, were peeled, cored and cut into thin slices. Then the fruit slices were threaded onto to string to dry out. Dried fruit was enjoyed during the winter by soaking and softening the fruit in boiling water. The leftover juice was drunk. Sometimes dried fruit was soaked in maple syrup and used to make a tasty pie.

Salting prevented fish and meat from spoiling. First, the meat or fish was cut into pieces and placed into barrels and generously covered with salt. Then salted water called brine was filled to the top of the barrel. The barrel was then covered and sealed. Meat, like salted pork, and fish, like salted herring, were delicious.

Smoking also prevented fish and meat from spoiling. First, meat or fish was salted, and dried before smoking. The meat or fish was hung up in the chimney away from the flames. The smoke from the fire cured or preserved the meat or fish. Another way to smoke the meat or fish was in a smokehouse. A smokehouse was a small log building with a fire pit inside, lined with stones. The meat or fish hung from the ceiling on ropes. To add flavour, special wood from hickory trees or green wood was burned. Pork and salmon were very tasty smoked.

Early settlers made fruits and vegetables last all year through preserving. Fruits were boiled, mixed with honey and cinnamon to make into sweet jams or jellies. Vinegars were made from apples, or other fruits. Vegetables like cucumbers and onions were pickled by preserving them in mixtures of vinegar, salt or other spices.

Thinking about: Preserving Food

Fill in the chart using information from the reading.

Foods that were smoked:	Foods that were pickled:	Foods that were dried:
Foods that were made into jams or jellies:	**Foods that were salted:**	**Foods that were made into vinegars:**

Why did early settlers preserve their foods in different ways?

_____

_____

_____

Comparing Pioneer Day Eating to Modern Day Eating

Meal	Pioneer Days Food like:	Modern Days Food like:
Breakfast	Bread Butter Porridge	
Lunch The Biggest Meal of the Day	Bread, butter and jelly Vegetables Meat Stew Soup Potatoes	
Dinner	Fried Pork Boiled Potatoes Corn Griddle Cakes Dandelion Root Coffee	
Snacks	Dried Apple Slices Jerky Pemmican Fruit	
Desserts	Pies	

In pioneer times almost all food was grown, and made from scratch. How have grocery stores changed life in modern days?

_____

_____

_____

Pioneer Dried Apple Treats

 Did you know fruits like apples were dried? Apples were cut into slices and threaded onto strings or thin sticks to hang near a fire to dry. During the winter the dried apple slices were soaked in water and enjoyed as a treat. Sometimes the apple slices were soaked in maple syrup then baked into apple pies.

What you need:

- A peeler
- 2 or 3 apples
- A paring knife
- Cookie sheets or Aluminum Foil
- An oven at 150 F

What you do:

1. With adult assistance, peel the apples and cut them into quarters.
2. Carefully remove the apple core and cut apple quarters into thin slices.
3. Place the apple slices on the cookie sheet or aluminum foil. Make sure there are spaces between each apple slice.
4. Using oven mitts, with an adult, place the cookie sheet into a heated oven to dry for at least five hours.
5. Make sure the apple slices dry evenly. Carefully flip them over with adult assistance and put them back into the oven.
6. Take two slices out of the oven and let cool. Begin to check if the apple slices are dried out and ready by gently squeezing them. If your fingers feel wet after squeezing them, the apple slices need to stay in the oven longer.
7. Once the apple slices are dried, store them in a tightly covered container or secured plastic bag.
8. Try your apple slices for a healthy snack.

Pioneer Butter Making

Did you know making butter was a good way for pioneers to make milk last? Churning milk made butter. First, fresh milk was left overnight in a shallow pan. The next morning the cream that rose to the surface of the milk would be skimmed off with a wooden spoon. The cream would then be left out until it was shiny and slightly sour. In the summer, the cream would only need to sit overnight. In the winter, the cream had to sit by the fire for several days.

When slightly shiny and sour, the cream was poured into a churn. Children usually had the chore of churning the butter. A churn looked like a small barrel. The dasher inside the churn, was a stick with paddles on the bottom. Children would beat the dasher in the churn up and down. The up and down motion of the dasher caused the cream to separate into buttermilk and small lumps of butter.

The buttermilk was poured out and saved for baking or feeding the animals. The butter was rinsed several times with cold water. After, the butter was pressed with a wooden spoon to get rid of the water. Then salt was added to the butter to keep it from spoiling.

Tell if the statements are true or false.

1. Churning milk makes butter.   True   False

2. Only adults churned butter in pioneer days.   True   False

3. A dasher was a stick with paddles on the top.   True   False

4. Salt was added to butter to keep it from spoiling.   True   False

4. Cream separated into buttermilk and butter.   True   False

5. In the summer, cream needed to sit for several days.   True   False

Thinking about: Pioneer Butter Making

Here are ten sentences. Number the sentences in order to explain how butter was made.

	Children would beat the dasher in the churn up and down.
	The next morning the cream that rose to the surface of the milk would be skimmed off with a wooden spoon.
	The buttermilk was poured out and saved for baking or feeding the animals.
	First, fresh milk was left overnight in a shallow pan.
	Then salt was added to the butter to keep it from spoiling.
	The up and down motion of the dasher caused the cream to separate into buttermilk and small lumps of butter.
	The butter was rinsed several times with cold water.
	The cream would then be left out until it was shiny and slightly sour.
	The butter was pressed with a wooden spoon to get rid of the water.
	When slightly shiny and sour, the cream was poured into a churn.

Pioneer Cheese

Did you know milk was hard to keep fresh in pioneer times? Pioneers would make cheese and butter as a way to make the milk last through the winter months. Cheese was usually made during the summer.

Here are the steps that a pioneer might have done to produce hard cheese.

1. The milk from the cows would be saved and let stand overnight.

2. The next morning, a small piece of rennet would be soaked in water. Rennet was made with the dried stomach of a newborn calf. Rennet makes the protein particles in milk clump together.

3. When the rennet water was ready, it was added to the milk.

4. After a short while, the milk would separate into curds and whey. Curds were the hard custard like bundles. Whey was the watery milk on top.

5. Next, the curds were cut up into cubes and were stirred with the whey over a small fire.

6. Once, the curds fell apart, the whey was strained off into a loosely woven basket lined with cheesecloth.

7. Then salt was added to the curds and stored in a cool place.

8. Over many months, the salted curds were pressed together using stones or bricks. This was called curing the cheese.

9. The cheese was ready to eat, once it was solid.

GeoWat innovative teacher publishing ©2003

Thinking about: Pioneer Cheese

Here are nine sentences.
Number the sentences in order to explain how cheese was made.

	Then salt was added to the curds and stored in a cool place.
	Next, the curds were cut up into cubes and were stirred with the whey over a small fire.
	Over many months, the salted curds were pressed together using stones or bricks.
	The next morning, a small piece of rennet would be soaked in water.
	The cheese was ready to eat, once it was solid.
	When the rennet water was ready, it was added to the milk.
	Once, the curds fell apart, the whey was strained off into a loosely woven basket lined with cheesecloth.
	The milk from the cows would be saved and let stand overnight.
	After a short while, the milk would separate into curds and whey.

Pioneer Villages

Did you know most pioneer villages were located on the shores of lakes or on the banks of rivers? Water was the simplest way to travel and to carry heavy supplies. Water was used for drinking, cooking and washing. Water provided power to run the gristmill or sawmill.

A pioneer community worked together to dam a nearby river and build a millpond. The flowing water from the millpond turned a waterwheel and provided power to run a gristmill or sawmill. A gristmill ground wheat and other grains into flour. A sawmill sawed logs into wooden planks or boards.

Businesses opened around the gristmill and sawmill. Some people opened shops that provided services such as a blacksmith, wainwright or harnessmaker. Other shops opened that provided goods. The general store sold key things like nails, spices and tools. Later on, doctors, lawyers and other professionals settled in the pioneer village. Since money was scarce, most people used a bartering system. Bartering means trading something in exchange for something else. For example, a pioneer could pay for the services of a blacksmith in exchange for a sack of flour.

Think about it!

1. On a separate piece of paper, create a labelled map of a pioneer village using crayons or coloured pencils.

2. Why was water important to a pioneer village?

_____

_____

_____

Thinking about: A Pioneer Village
Compare the buildings found in a pioneer village to your community.

Buildings in a pioneer village:	Buildings in your community:

1. How is a pioneer village the same as your community?

_____

_____

2. How is a pioneer village different from your community?

_____

_____

_____

The General Store

Did you know the general store was a very important place for pioneers? For the most part, pioneers had to make everything they needed. Once general stores were set up in some villages, people came from far away to pick up supplies.

The general store was usually a two-storey building with two large display windows in the front. A hitching post was stationed at the front of the general store. Pioneers could tie up their horses while they shopped. Inside, the general store was packed with both dry goods and wet goods.

The storekeeper ordered goods from larger towns or cities. Some special goods like china came from as far away as Europe. The goods were delivered by wagon or boat. The storekeeper kept a record of each pioneer's account in a ledger. Since money was scarce, most people traded or bartered things they had grown or made on their farm. For example, a pioneer might trade butter for some fabric.

The storekeeper stocked many types of products. Salt for preserving, spices for cooking, tools for farming were things a pioneer could find at the general store. If the pioneer had extra money to spend, they could buy things like buttons, fabric, ribbon, china dishes, candy or school supplies.

The general store was a meeting place for early settlers. It was a chance to get to know and meet new neighbours and to catch up on the latest news. Sometimes, a newspaper from the city would be posted. Sometimes people even played games like checkers.

Often villages grew around the general store. People opened up shops and services that pioneers might need. These included the blacksmith, wainwright, milner and baker.

Thinking about: The General Store

A. Connect the phrases to make true sentences.

1. The general store was	many types of products.
2. The general store was packed	by wagon or boat.
3. The storekeeper stocked	a meeting place for early settlers.
4. The storekeeper kept a record	with both dry goods and wet goods.
5. The goods were delivered	from larger towns or cities.
6. The storekeeper ordered goods	of each pioneer's account in a ledger.

B. Answer the following questions using information from the reading.

1. The general store was a meeting place for settlers. Explain.

_____

_____

_____

2. How did people pay the storekeeper?

_____

3. List three things a pioneer could buy at the general store.

_____ _____ _____

Pioneer Occupations

Did you know an apprentice was someone learning a trade? Many tradesmen would take on a child apprentice to teach them a trade. Apprentices learned on the job. It usually took four to seven years of training to become a tradesman such as a blacksmith or a wainwright. Here is a list of some early pioneer occupations.

Blacksmith

Did you know the blacksmith had the important job of fitting oxen and horses with iron shoes? Iron shoes kept the hooves of these working animals from wearing away. The blacksmith also made iron tools like hoes, rakes, spades, scythes and sickles. Other items the blacksmith crafted included sleigh runners, plows, nails, knives and even guns.

Wainwright

Did you know wainwrights were carriage makers? They built the top part of carriages, wagons sleighs and coaches using hardwoods such as oak, and elm. Wainwrights then hired other tradesmen like wheelwrights, blacksmiths, painters and woodworkers to complete the rest of the carriage.

Wheelwright

Did you know wheelwrights crafted many sizes of wheels for carriages, wagons, carts, and wheelbarrows? These wheels were constructed with wooden hubs, spokes and rim. Then an iron ring called a tire was put around the outer part of the wheel to make it sturdy.

Cooper

Did you know a coop is a kind of wooden container? The cooper in the village was the person who made barrels and kegs to store liquids and dry items. Coopers also crafted household items like pails, buckets, butter churns and wash tubs.

Early Pioneer Occupations

Shoemaker

Did you know the foot shapes that shoemakers carved were called lasts? The shoemaker used a last to help shape a piece of leather into a boot or shoe. Lasts came in three sizes: small, medium and large. Usually shoemakers made a child's pair of shoes a bit big, so that a child could grow into them. To make the shoes fit; rags would be stuffed into their shoes.

Harness Maker

Did you know harness makers were also called saddle makers? A harness maker was someone who carefully crafted leather harnesses and saddles for large animals like cows and horses.

Think about it!

Write a sentence to tell about each of these pioneer occupations.

Apprentice _____

Blacksmith _____

_____

Wainwright _____

_____

Wheelwright _____

_____

Cooper _____

_____

Shoemaker _____

_____

Harness maker_____

Pioneer School Time

Did you know in early pioneer days children went to school in a one-room schoolhouse? At first, many children did not go to school and learned what they could from their parents. Over time as villages grew, the community would work together to build a schoolhouse.

Inside the one-room schoolhouse there were benches made of wooden planks and narrow tables. This is where the children sat. The teacher's desk faced the students. In the centre of the room was a large boxwood stove or fireplace to heat the room. Usually a student started the fire each morning. There was little else in the schoolhouse. All the grades were in the same class.

A male teacher was called a schoolmaster. A female teacher was called a schoolmistress. The families of the students paid the teacher's salary. Sometimes teachers were paid with money. Sometimes teachers were paid with things made on a farm like a bag of flour or cured ham. Sometimes teachers lived with a family for a period as payment.

Teachers were very strict. Teachers kept a birch rod or stick to whack children's hands if they did not listen. Students had to memorize and recite everything they learned. The teacher taught the three "R"s: reading, "riting" and "rithematic." This was another way of saying reading, writing and math.

In early schools, students had a slate board and a slate pencil. Later on, students wrote on paper using a quill pen. A quill pen was made from the large feathers of a goose. A knife was used to sharpen the end of the quill to make a point to dip into ink.

Students would attend school six days a week. Some older students did not attend school regularly so they could help with planting and harvesting on the farm.

GeoWat innovative teacher publishing ©2003

Thinking about: Pioneer School Time

Connect the phrases to make true sentences.

1. In the centre of the room was   with things made on a farm.

2. All the grades were   a slate board and a slate pencil.

3. A quill pen was made   was a large boxwood stove or fireplace.

4. In early schools, students had   in the same class.

5. Sometimes teachers were paid   from the large feathers of a goose.

Using information from the reading, and your own ideas fill in the chart.

Ways school was the same….	Ways school was different…

Would you want to have attended school during pioneer times? Explain your thinking.

_____

_____

_____

Homemade Fiddle

Did you know early settlers made their own instruments? They had many ways of creating instruments that would provide the rhythm and beat needed for a barn dance. Banjos were made from dried gourds and fiddles were made from a string and stick. In the following activity, create your own homemade fiddle or "sound bow".

What you need:
- A hammer
- A large empty can with one end-cap removed
- Scissors
- Heavy string
- A pencil

What you do:

1. With adult assistance, punch a hoe in the middle of the bottom of the can using a hammer and a nail.
2. Next, cut a length of heavy string from your waist to the floor.
3. Carefully tie a large knot at one of the string and thread it through the hole in the can. The large knot should catch on the inside of the can.
4. Tie the other end of the heavy string around the middle of the short stick, ruler or pencil.
5. Your instrument is ready to play. Place the can on the floor and hold it in place by putting your foot on top of it.
6. Next, curl your fingers around the short stick or pencil and pull the heavy string nice and tight.
7. Pluck the string using a finger from your other hand.
8. Experiment with the sounds you can, by loosening or tightening the string.

People and Places In A Pioneer Village

```
U  J  A  S  F  H  T  S  A  W  M  I  L  L  W  G
F  G  S  T  O  R  E  K  E  E  P  E  R  I  E  E
D  R  E  S  S  M  A  K  E  R  O  U  X  S  A  N
P  X  A  Q  N  N  C  O  O  P  E  R  D  M  V  E
Y  A  S  F  W  E  H  R  T  Z  F  R  Z  I  E  R
S  A  M  F  Z  P  E  D  L  A  R  V  S  N  R  A
I  M  I  L  L  E  R  O  U  X  A  C  W  I  Z  L
L  X  E  T  T  U  Y  V  T  Y  N  Z  A  S  S  S
V  E  V  R  Z  B  L  A  C  K  S  M  I  T  H  T
E  Z  A  R  C  Q  S  D  G  J  L  P  N  E  O  O
R  W  H  E  E  L  W  R  I  G  H  T  W  R  E  R
S  Z  T  X  J  H  F  S  A  L  F  S  R  H  M  E
M  G  R  I  S  T  M  I  L  L  H  K  I  B  A  E
I  U  Q  G  H  B  K  E  R  R  T  Y  G  F  K  R
T  U  E  R  T  Y  U  I  O  P  I  U  H  O  E  T
H  A  R  N  E  S  S  M  A  K  E  R  T  I  R  Y
```

Blacksmith	Dressmaker	Gristmill
Wainwright	Minister	Harness maker
Wheelwright	Miller	General store
Storekeeper	Silversmith	Sawmill
Teacher	Cooper	Pedlar
Shoemaker	Weaver	

Unscramble the following people and places in a pioneer village.

llmistgri _____   ralepd _____

rcheeat _____   reveaw _____

preoco _____   eeoreprestk _____

skcthimbal _____   rekamsesrd _____

Pioneer Farm Animals and Crops

```
P E A L K E C R Q U G R T U X D
C C A T H P D O L T C E N H C O
P O T A T O Z D R Y U O E D V G
Z W B L S A E S E N C R U S F H
S N H O R S E J C B U P Y D E F
Q L M X S H E E P V M A R S H A
H A P V G S Z L U B B O X E N S
O M M N H Q I O M H E P S G K H
G B F D J U Z J P Y R O A B J E
S E W H E A T G K T U R N I P N
L M N C K S D H I F O N I O N O
K R Y E L H Z C N C X H J F H U
D U C K G P L O H L B A R L E Y
J I O E Z T V C A B B A G E P I
B E A N X E R T U T C A R R O T
G R O O S T E R I F S E R T Y D
```

Wheat	Potato	Geese	Dog
Pumpkin	Corn	Hogs	Cat
Bean	Cow	Onion	Rooster
Squash	Oxen	Cabbage	Lamb
Barley	Sheep	Duck	Turnip
Oats	Hen	Horse	Pea
Carrot	Cucumber	Rye	

Comparing Pioneer and Modern Day Family Chores

Fill in the chart and discuss your findings.

Family Member	Examples of Responsibilities In Pioneer Times:	Examples of Responsibilities In Modern Times:
Men and Older Boys	<ul><li>Clearing the land</li><li>Cutting trees for lumber</li><li>Building a home</li><li>Removing stoves from fields</li><li>Ploughing fields</li><li>Planting Crops</li><li>Harvesting Crops</li><li>Hunting</li><li>Shearing Sheep</li><li>Building Fences</li><li>Making Furniture</li><li>Digging wells</li></ul>	
Women and Older Girls	<ul><li>Taking care of the children</li><li>Taking care of livestock</li><li>Making warm clothes, blankets</li><li>Preparing meals</li><li>Preserving and storing food</li><li>Planting Crops</li><li>Making Candles</li><li>Helping with the harvest</li></ul>	
Young Girls	<ul><li>Helping take care of younger siblings</li><li>Feeding livestock</li><li>Washing Dishes</li></ul>	
Young Boys	<ul><li>Gathering firewood</li><li>Feeding and tending livestock</li><li>Helping with the harvest</li></ul>	

Pioneer Farm Crops

Did you know planting crops took much time and great effort all year round, by the whole family? The land was cleared and prepared for planting. Seeds like wheat, oat, corn and barley were planted. Then, pioneers waited over time, hoping for a good mixture of weather so their crops could grow. When ripe, the crops were harvested and milled.

Step One: Clearing the Land

The land was cleared of any trees, roots, stumps or large rocks. Then using a hoe, the hard soil was broken apart. Sometimes oxen or horses were used to pull a plough to break up the earth. The plough had a sharp blade that cut into the earth and turned it over.

Step Two: Sowing the Seeds

Usually around the month of May seeds like wheat, oats, corn and barley were sowed. Fistful of seeds were scattered by hand to the right and left as the farmer walked through the field. This was called **broadcasting**. Although broadcasting wasted many seeds, it was still the best to sow seeds.

Step Three: Covering the Seeds

A large branch was attached to an ox's yoke. The ox dragged the branch through the field spreading the soil over the seeds. Now the pioneers waited, hoping for a good mixture of weather so their crops could grow.

Pioneer Crops

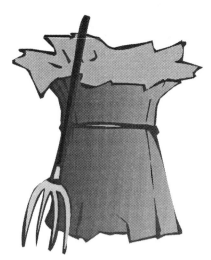

Step Four: Harvesting the Crop

In the fall, crops were harvested when the moon was full. The moon provided extra light so farmers could work longer. First, the crop was cut with sharp curved knives called **sickles** or scythes. As one person cut the grain, another person followed to gather and bind the grain into bundles called **sheaves**. When ten bundles of sheaves were put together, it was called a **stook**. The stooks were stored in a dry safe place like a barn for protection from the weather. Harvesting bees were held to help harvest crops.

Step Five: Threshing

Before the harvested crops could be milled, the grain had to be threshed. **Threshing** separated the grain seeds from the stalk. A farmer did this by spreading bundles of grain on the barn floor and beating the heads of the grain using a flail. A **flail** was a tool made of two sticks loosely fastened together by a chain. As the flail struck the grain, seeds or kernels were freed, and fell off the stalk.

Step Six: Winnowing

After being threshed, the grain needed to be separated from the tiny pieces of useless seed head called chaff. To do this the grain was winnowed. **Winnowing** was when the grain and chaff were placed in a big wooden tray and shaken. The heavy grain would fall and remain ready to go to the gristmill. Meanwhile the light chaff would blow away.

Thinking about: Farming Crops

Name _____

1. List four types of farm crops.

_____   _____

_____   _____

2. Find the definitions of the bolded words using the information from the reading.

Broadcasting _____

Sickle _____

Sheaves _____

Stook _____

Threshing _____

Flail _____

Winnowing _____

Here are the six steps to farming crops. Name a tool or farming method used for each step.

1. **Step One: Clearing the Land** _____

2. **Step Two: Sowing the Seeds** _____

3. **Step Three: Covering the Seeds** _____

4. **Step Four: Harvesting the Crop** _____

5. **Step Five: Threshing** _____

6. **Step Six: Winnowing** _____

The Gristmill: Grinding Grain Into Flour

Did you know grain that is good enough to be ground into flour is called grist? A gristmill was a building where large quantities of kernels of grain could be crushed between big flat stones and made into flour. Flour is used to make bread. It would take many difficult hours for a pioneer to grind grain by hand to make flour. The gristmill saved pioneers many hours of work.

Gristmills were built close to water and run by a person called a miller. A miller's job was to grind the grain and to make sure the gristmill ran smoothly. A miller was usually paid a part of each pioneer's flour as payment.

To make the gristmill run, water was made to flow down a wooden trough and into the blades of a large wooden wheel. The running water made the wooden wheel turn. At the same, a shaft connected to a large heavy stone wheel called a millstone turned. The millstone rotated around the top of another stone that did not move called a bedstone.

Meanwhile, grain was poured into a funnel called a hopper. The pouring grain tumbled along the grooves between the millstones and was ground. Wheat was ground into flour. Corn was ground into cornmeal.

1. What was a gristmill?

_____

2. Why was the gristmill important to pioneers?

_____

3. How was the miller paid?

_____

Name _____

Thinking about the Gristmill: Grinding Grain Into Flour

Fill in the blanks with the correct word. Use information from the reading to help you.

To make the gristmill run, _____ was made to flow

down a _____ and into the blades of a large

wooden _____. The running water made the

wooden wheel turn.   At the same, a _____

connected to a large heavy stone wheel called a _____

turned. The millstone rotated around the top of another stone

that did not move called a _____.

Meanwhile, grain was poured into a _____

called a hopper.   The pouring _____ tumbled

along the _____ between the millstones and was

ground. _____ was ground into flour. Corn

was ground into _____.

Word box

wooden trough	bedstone	grain	funnel	shaft
wheat	cornmeal	water	millstone	grooves

Spinning Flax Thread

 Did you know some pioneers grew a special plant used to make thread? This special grassy plant was called flax. First, the stalks of flax were soaked and flattened. Next, plant fibres were spun into thread. Spinning is the action of pulling and twisting the fibres. One type of fine thread made from flax was called linen. The second type of thread made from flax was a coarse thread called tow. In the following activity finger spin your own thread.

What you need:
- Cotton balls
- Strong fingers

What you do:
1. Hold the cotton ball in your hand lightly grasping it between your thumb and index finger.
2. Next, begin to slowly pull out the fibres in the cotton ball using your other thumb, and index finger.
3. Make sure you twist the cotton fibres evenly as they are carefully pulled.
4. Watch how the thread forms.

Think about it!
Fill in the blanks with the correct word from the reading.

1. Pioneers grew a special grassy plant called _____.

2. First, the stalks of flax were _____ and flattened.

3. Next, plant fibres were _____ into thread.

4. _____ is the action of pulling and twisting the fibres.

5. One type of fine thread made from flax was called_____.

6. The second type of thread was a coarse thread called _____.

Sheep Wool

Name _____

Did you know sheep were raised to provide wool to make yarn and cloth? When ready, the sheep's fleece was sheared or shaved off, and the raw wool was washed. Next, the wool from the fleece was combed and brushed to untangle the fibres. This was called carding. After that, a spinning wheel spun the sheep wool into yarn by pulling and twisting it evenly.

Some of the yarn was used for knitting. The women and girls in the family knit shawls, scarves, socks, mittens, caps, stockings and sweaters. The yarn was also used to make warm blankets and rugs.

Some of the yarn was woven into cloth using a large loom. The cloth was used to make clothing for the whole pioneer family. Often, pioneers dyed the cloth different colours using flowers, leaves, bark and berries. Women and girls used the cloth to sew dresses as well as to make pants and shirts for the men and boys. Leftover scraps of cloth or old worn out cloth from clothes were used to make patchwork quilts and rag rugs.

Think about it!

1. Number the sentences to show how to make sheep wool.

	The wool from the fleece was brushed and untangled.
	A spinning wheel spun the sheep wool into yarn.
	The sheep's fleece was sheared and the raw wool washed.

2. List ways the sheep wool was used.

_____

_____

_____

Pioneer Paper Quilt

Keep special memories alive by creating a quilt in the pioneer tradition.

What you need:
- Colouring materials
- Paper Squares
- Yarn
- Hole punch
- Pencil
- Ruler

What to do:

1. Brainstorm a list with the children of reasons for which they could be thankful.
2. Demonstrate for the children how to create a border, a ruler's width around four paper square;
3. Model for the children how to create a cross- stitch pattern with crayon inside the border.
4. In the centre of two squares, instruct children to draw a picture of something for which they are thankful;
5. In the other two squares instruct children to print words or phrases of why they are thankful;
6. Next, model for the children how to punch holes through all four squares around the edges;
7. Using yarn, instruct children to lace together their paper squares to form a quilt.

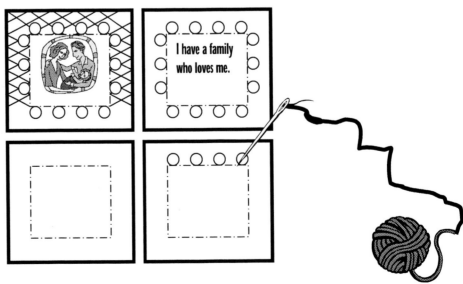

Canada's Pioneers Activity Cards

Pioneer Activity Card
Research Poster

Create a research poster that describes step-by-step direction of how something was done in pioneer times. For example:

- ❖ How a gristmill operated.
- ❖ How to make butter.
- ❖ How to make cheese.
- ❖ How to clear land.
- ❖ Your Choice.

Poster Requirements:
- ❖ Large neat printing with a clear title.
- ❖ Labelled drawing or diagram.
- ❖ Steps and details clearly written in complete sentences.
- ❖ Explain its importance in pioneer life.

Pioneer Activity Card
Pioneer Letter

Write a letter to a friend pretending you are an early settler starting a new life in Canada.

Make sure your letter includes details about:
- ❖ Where you are originally from and why you came to Canada?
- ❖ What your age is and the types of chores you do?
- ❖ The best part about living in Canada.
- ❖ The worst part about living in Canada.

Other Requirements:
- ❖ Make sure your letter starts with a salutation i.e. Dear_____,
- ❖ Sentences are complete with correct punctuation.
- ❖ Printing is neat.

Canada's Pioneers Activity Cards

Pioneer Activity Card
Pioneer Cinquain Poem

A cinquain poem is a five-line poem. Create a cinquain poem about a Canadian pioneer.

- ❖ Line1- one word title i.e. pioneer
- ❖ Line 2- two words to describe the title
- ❖ Line 3- three words which describe actions
- ❖ Line 4- four words to express feelings
- ❖ Line 5- repeat line 1

Requirements:
- ❖ Large neat printing
- ❖ Check for spelling
- ❖ Use descriptive vocabulary

Pioneer Activity Card
Build a Log Cabin

An early settler's first home was usually a log cabin. Try building your own.

What you need:
- ❖ Popsicle sticks
- ❖ Toothpicks
- ❖ Plastiscene
- ❖ Glue

What you do:
Using any of the above materials build a one-room log cabin.

Challenge:
1. Cut a piece of paper to fit inside your cabin.
2. On the paper, draw a floor plan of what would be inside the cabin, like the hearth.

Pioneer Activity Card
Pioneer Stenciling

Pioneers liked to decorate their homes using stencils. Stencils are design and shape cutouts that you paint inside. When you lift the stencil, the design or shape can be seen.

What you need:
- ❖ Paint and paintbrush
- ❖ Stiff paper
- ❖ Something to decorate like paper, or a box
- ❖ Scissors
- ❖ Pencil

What you do:
1. Carefully, cut out a simple shape on the stiff paper.
2. Place the stiff paper shape on what you want to decorate.
3. Pounce the paint inside of the cutout shape onto what you want to decorate.
4. Create a pattern

Pioneer Activity Card
Make Your Own Butter

In the following activity, make your own tasty butter. Smother some butter on fresh bread and taste!

What you need:
- ▪ 1 cup whipping cream
- ▪ A wooden spoon
- ▪ Small jar with lid
- ▪ A bowl

What you do:
1. Carefully pour the whipping cream into the jar.
2. Next, tightly attach the jar lid and shake the jar briskly for at least 10 minutes.
3. Watch how the whipping cream separates into two parts. One part is buttermilk. One part is made of yellow lumps or the butter.
4. Carefully, pour out the butter and buttermilk.
5. Rinse the butter with cold water.
6. Using the wooden spoon, press the butter against the side of the jar.
7. Taste the butter!

Canada's Pioneers Home Study

Dear Parents and Guardians,

In this Canada's Pioneers home study, your child will have the opportunity to compare the lifestyle of a pioneer to his or her own daily life at home.

While completing the home study, encourage your child to think about how their life is similar or different to a pioneer.

In addition, try one or more of the following pioneer home challenges to get a taste of pioneer life.

- ❖ Spend an evening at home without using electricity. Use candles for lightning.
- ❖ Do household chores like washing dishes without using a dishwasher.
- ❖ Tell stories, read, or play board games.
- ❖ Braid strips of cloth. Arrange the braid into a circle and tack together with thread to make a hot plate.
- ❖ Eat a pioneer meal with things like stew, boiled vegetables, apple pie, bread with butter, honey and pickled vegetables.
- ❖ Do an Internet search on your local area and find who the first people were to settle in your area.

Your family's participation is greatly appreciated!

_____

Name _____

Comparing Pioneer times to Modern Times Home Study

Pioneer	Your Family	Same	Different
Pioneers made their clothes using homespun cloth.	Where do you get your clothes?		
Pioneers grew their own food.	Where do you get your food?		
Sometimes Pioneers bought things at the general store.	Do you buy things from a store?		
A pioneer's main meal of the day was lunch.	What is your main meal of the day?		
A pioneer family usually lived in a home they built themselves.	Did your family build your home?		
Many pioneers lived on a farm.	Where do you live?		
Pioneer children had chores to do at home.	Do you have to do chores?		
Pioneers made their own medicine.	Where does your family get medicine?		
Pioneer children went to school in a one room schoolhouse.	Does your school only have one room?		
Pioneers washed the dishes by hand.	How do you wash dishes?		
Pioneers used candles and lanterns to light their homes.	How do you light your home?		
Pioneers did most of their cooking using the fire from the fireplace.	What do you use to do your cooking?		
Pioneers stored their food using icehouses, root cellars and springhouses.	How do you store food to keep it fresh?		

Comparing Pioneer times to Modern Times Home Study

1. Look at the information you gathered on the chart. Are you
   similar to a pioneer's way of life or different? Explain.

_____

_____

_____

_____

_____

2. Name modern things that pioneers did not have. Tell how they
   make life easier and save time.

Modern Thing	How does it save time or makes life easier.
Car	You can travel distances faster and save time

Canada's Pioneers Unit Test

1. Tell two reasons people wanted to come settle in Canada.

_____

_____

_____

2. Explain why it was difficult for a settler to clear the land.

_____

_____

_____

3. Name four countries people came from to settle in Canada.

_____   _____

_____   _____

4. Number the sentences to show how to make sheep wool.

	The wool from the fleece was brushed and untangled.
	A spinning wheel spun the sheep wool into yarn.
	The sheep's fleece was sheared and the raw wool washed.

5. List two ways sheep wool was used.

_____

_____

_____

Canada's Pioneers Unit Test

6. One of the biggest hurdles for pioneers, was to make food last through out the seasons. Explain.

_____

_____

_____

7. Tell if the statement is true or false.

Aboriginal peoples showed pioneers how to make toboggans.   True   False

Early settlers were used to cold winters.   True   False

Aboriginal peoples did not like to trade goods.   True   False

Many Aboriginal peoples were expert farmers and helped pioneers how to best use the land.   True   False

Aboriginal peoples helped pioneers cope with illness.   True   False

Canada's Pioneers Unit Test

8. Write a sentence to tell about each of these pioneer occupations.

Apprentice _____

Blacksmith _____

_____

Wainwright _____

_____

9. Write five things you have learned about pioneers.

_____

_____

_____

_____

_____

_____

Self- Evaluation: **What I did in the unit.**

The best part of the unit was……

_____

_____

_____

I learned about……..

_____

_____

_____

I want to learn more about….

_____

_____

_____

My Work Habits:

	Yes	Sometimes	I need to try harder.
I listened to the teacher			
I tried my best to work on my own			
I did neat work with lots of details			
I was a good group member			

Rubric for Student Self-Assessment

A	WOW!	✓ I completed my work independently on time and with care. ✓ I added details and followed the instructions without help. ✓ I understand and can talk about what I have learned.
B	BRAVO	✓ I completed my work on time and with care. ✓ I followed the instructions with almost no help. ✓ I understand and can talk about what I have learned.
C	OKAY	✓ I completed my work. ✓ I followed the instructions with some help. ✓ I understand and can talk about most of what I have learned.
D	UH-OH	✓ I need to complete my work on time and with care. ✓ I should ask for help when I need it. ✓ I understand and can talk about a few of the things that I have learned.

Post the above rubric in your classroom to assist children in self- evaluation and direction for improvement in completing the tasks assigned.

Student Assessment Rubric

	Level One	Level Two	Level Three	Level Four
B A S I C C O N C E P T S	• Shows little of understanding of concepts. • Rarely gives complete explanations. • Teacher support is intensive.	• Shows some understanding of concepts. • Gives appropriate, but incomplete explanations. • Some teacher assistance is needed.	• Shows understanding of most concepts. • Usually gives complete or nearly complete explanations. • Infrequent teacher support is needed.	• Shows understanding of all or almost all concepts • Consistently gives appropriate and complete explanations independently. • No teacher support is needed.
C O M M U N I C A T I O N	• Rarely communicates with clarity and precision in written and oral work • Rarely uses appropriate terminology and vocabulary • Intensive teacher prompts needed to use correct vocabulary	• Sometimes communicates with clarity and precision in written and oral work • Rarely uses appropriate terminology and vocabulary • Occasional teacher prompts needed to use correct vocabulary	• Usually communicates with clarity and precision in written and oral work • Usually uses appropriate terminology and vocabulary • Infrequent teacher prompts needed to use correct vocabulary	• Consistently communicates with clarity and precision in written and oral work with supporting details • Consistently uses appropriate terminology and vocabulary • No teacher prompts needed to use correct vocabulary
C O N C E P T A P P L I C A T I O N	• Student displays little understanding of connecting and comparing pioneer living to present day living. • Rarely applies concepts and skills in a variety of contexts • Intensive teacher support is needed to encourage application of concepts	• Student sometimes displays understanding of connecting and comparing pioneer living to present day living. • Sometimes applies concepts and skills in a variety of contexts • Occasional teacher support is needed to encourage application of concepts	• Student usually displays understanding of connecting and comparing pioneer living to present day living. • Usually applies concepts and skills in a variety of contexts • Infrequent teacher support is needed to encourage application of concepts	• Student consistently displays understanding of connecting and ·comparing pioneer living to present day living. • Almost always applies concepts and skills in a variety of contexts • No teacher support is needed to · encourage application of concepts

Name _____

Student Evaluation Sheet

Activity Completed	Grade

Teacher Comments:

_____

_____

_____

Canadian Pioneer Expert

CONGRATULATIONS TO

ON THE COMPLETION OF THE PIONEER HOME STUDY

Canadian Pioneer Expert

Quality Worker

★ ★ ★ ★ ★ ★ ★